The Best of
Mijikai Haiku

edited by Ed Bremson

Mijikai Press

Printed in the United States of America
First Printing, 2014
ISBN-13: 978-0692233870
Mijikai Press
2901 Old Orchard Road
Raleigh, NC 27607

www.facebook.com/MijikaiPress

Introduction 2012

Mijikai Haiku means short or brief haiku. It is also the name of a Facebook group that I started September 26, 2012, with help from my Vietnamese poet friend Vo Tuan Hoang Vy (who gave me the name for the group). In the past few short months our numbers have grown to more than one hundred members – from such diverse locations as Vietnam, Mongolia, Punjab, India, Japan, Turkey, Russia, Croatia, Denmark, Canada, California, Arkansas, and North Carolina – and we have written and posted many hundreds of Mijikai Haiku. Here we present to you just a sampling of our posts: 205 poems from 51 poets. We hope you enjoy what we have done. Perhaps you will find yourself wanting to write Mijikai Haiku yourself.

Ed Bremson

spring –
crosswalk signals
chirping

on my table –
Buddha
with his back turned

women and birds
their morning songs

cobwebs
catch moonlight
but can't hold it

Vo Tuan Hoang Vy

Silver boat
in moon waves
a lonely moth.

Dusk
too bright
an empty sky.

A dewdrop
Falling
From a lotus bud.

Roses
in sunlight . . .
their young color.

Sandi Pray

train whistle . .
rearranging
darkness

bat . . .
to and from
the moon

the trail
of your touch . .
falling leaf

new moon . .
in every corner
darkness

Traci Siler

lips
dripping
moonbeams

cookie
moon
crumbles

the blush
on her cheek
November

mapping your skin
lost and found

Rosie Mann

warm sunrays
through sheer curtains
dove calls

stars twinkle
in the bird-bath
winter chill

autumn breeze
rose petals
in a puddle

sequins
on her stole
winter moon

Arvinder Kaur

ripples
after the immersion
stillness

evening aarti
incense
mist

crayons
little girl
pink toes

blue jacaranda
full bloom
daughter's smile

Veronika Zora Novak

balloons...
the cosmos
breathes

barren branches...
bird song
unravels

a cricket's
serenade...
silent heat

snowflakes...
the warmth of
my hand

Pat Geyer

indifference
not different
just hurts

kit
car
son of a gun

black
Friday
night lights

red berry
blue berry
jam with chrome

Tuvshinzaya Nergui

eagle...
flying high
earth!

musing…
fragile leaves
falling

beggar-
a time
stopped

time-
a king
d'être

Vibeke Laier

playing
with stars
life line dance

spider's web
red apples
autumn rain

morning splash
single
duckling

as water
in silverlight--
your kiss

Joan Barrett Roberts

I see deep
into these
autumn woods

always now
forever
singing

winter
fleece robe
bare shoulders

light of my day
a shadowed wall
on sunbeams

Sheila Windsor

fog
fox
fog

hungry exit

the whole slaughterhouse screams

trees sing back

Kris Kennedy

night
stolen
no winks

light
- love
in the dark

racing
my heart
before the start

snow blanket
warms
my heart

Linda L. Ashok

drops
of words
dawn

a cry
the burst of
blossom

needling
tears
my mom

biting
the last
song

Sondra J. Byrnes

morning sky
a frown
of clouds

in a blink
the moon turns
on

making space
for emptiness

meditation
a nonself
drifting

Stevie Strang

sleepless
night
daybreak

autumn
rain
orange

the scent
of you
apple pie

black
Friday
red

Asni Amin

wind song
taking me
wherever

in a breath …
colors
of sunset

in boxes –
dreams
unraveling

softly
in silence ...
first leaf

Stephano Brighi

October sun ...
contrasts -
energy press

absorb light
explode ... then write
tracks - my tracks

in hot wind
a fragment streamlined
plows thought

Date back light,
I welcome my memories
..... dilute fears

Orrin PreJean

greeting him
hand-painted
hallelujahs

cajun sky
smell
of marshes

creole moon
ancestral house shudders

a morning song—
...stumbling over his shoes

Tony Piccini

Naked,
crazy eyes
of eternity

Fear,
shell of the fruit

A trench -
two defeats

OM -
link

Dawn Apanius

knitting
afternoon
softness

windy
night
chimes

owl flight
questions
for my ancestors

snowdrifts
another variation
of chicken soup

Kayo Mizutani

owl's eye
deep forest
midnight dream

bookmark
pressed flower
autumn sunlight

detour
bush clover flowers
on the roadside

a ladybug
on the rainbow
my dream...

Freddy Ben-Arroyo

dusty path -
where to
ant?

high heeling long legged beauty

spam retrieved love letter

Bogie's hat and I'll star film noir

RD McManes

sunrise
night fades
gray

clouds
leaking
moonlight

autumn
colors
swirl

sunset
warm glow
falls

Carole Johnston

night walk
still magic
without you

gone
Jersey Shore
no zen

haiku
happens
dog walk

lost
on the road
bliss

Mary Hohlman

flowers
spilling
stars

autumn wind
rapids
and butterflies

mint
moon
her kiss

the stars
my wine
sublime

Christine L. Villa

autumn skies
words just
tumble down

I fall
to pieces . . .
rain puddles

our dreams
unfolding . . .
cherry buds

summer clouds
my thoughts
reshaping

Kath Abela Wilson

silk floss
elephant back scratcher

on one branch
two

pop-up koi
lily leaf head

mint hedge
shoulder rub

Christina Nguyen

broken
sky raining
love

his death
her pregnancy
tears

full moon
midday
somewhere

silence
unfolding
night

N.E. Taylor

rachmaninoff
prelude
dancing water

shoes
red only
for him

red
hibiscus
holiday

lotus
lost moon
drifting

Gillena Cox; T&T

the grackle
on the wall -
a young bird

the park
the people
Divali festivities

bright sunshine
the yellow
crayon

garden
walk
white butterfly

John Mcdonald

crocuses springing

spring
greening
the stream

autumn -
the beehive's pulse
slowing down

first grandchild -
swifts tying bows
over the gift

Carole Harrison

lightning ...
space between
raindrops

old man
his shadow
salutes

deserted playground
stillness
ghostly shadow

lavender
childhood
returning

Gary Blankenship

turtle island
salamander moon

beneath
silk robes
unbleached cotton

a leaf hangs
on the gutter's edge

my forever
nearly
passed

Dalvir Gill

cloths-line
shooting-star
ebony

light house in
oceanic fog –
firefly

gross
subtle
isingness

thunder
quiet after
the spat

Tiburcio Samsa

My blessing
may your life
blossom

A word
thrown into a pond
waves

A kiss
love's dew
on the cheek

Beaches of Pattaya
bitches on the shore

Ernesto P. Santiago

good night
green grass
still green

blinking
your way
night star

sun still
bleeds red--
old pen

red bumps...
swiftly come for me
oh, God!

Jayashree Maniyil

frost bite...
a baby
teething

bald patch...
my backyard
lawn

their first
burnt meal...
newly wed

silent
in my grave...
he is late again

Alegria 'Alee' Imperial

attic
ships lost
on my watch

Spanish fir
drips
off night

pine scent
half
a secret

rain mist
our steps
moonless

Kris Kondo

paring
it down~
pear

brain-scan...
of someone who craves
persimmons

mood green
this budding
morning

fish tank...
who is watching
who ?

Ivan I. Ivančan

little snail...
a trip
up the blade

lake...
a fish jumps out
of a cloud

hill-slope...
tractor ploughing
the horizon

blackout
cigs walking
the pavement

Brendan McNassar

Snow crystals
Fleeting
Presumption

Father
graveyard
Son

blades
edges cuts
verdant

garlic kiss
sensation
lasting

Kathy Uyen Nguyen

pillow talk—
your dreams
eclipse mine

pine dew
trembling
a vireo's call

duck-feathered path . . .
I too shed
my past

I question
my upbringing . . .
tree pose

Chris Ziesler

this tired world
asleep
under snow's comforter

half-frozen pond
wild geese
songs fade southwards

dank winter fog
zen café
one teapot brewing

winter desert wakes
cool haze of dew
a cactus flowers

Gennady Nov

raindrops
mixed with make-up
taste bitter

autumn wind
no signs
of mosquitoes

night
throbbing through
silence

itinerant sleep
into
wisps of cloud

Ayşen Gacan Gülbağ

Look
leaf by rain
falls

sound of leaves
best of
lullabies

fall's
quinces—
shorter days

white hair-
traces of autumn
defoliation

Nadalsuren Purevdorj

blues...
flowing in middle
full moons

flowers
do not want
farewell

mist
embraces mountains—
autumn

chill...
lingering
cheek

Azucena Leon

whispering elm
hiding my voice

equipment for winter,
weightless love

Little turtle
walks
without maps

Poems fed
washing dishes

Daniel Gahnertz

barflies
like fireflies
but full of lies

bridge opening
the cyclists
yawn

taking photos
of tourists
taking photos

foggy bridge
a tram
floats

Tomislav Maretić

swells -
seagulls now visible,
now hidden

sounds in night...
a mouse on
my guitar

headlights –
a cat's eyes
hopping

applause –
panting bellies of
girl dancers

Dubravko Ivančan (1931 - 1981)

Sunset... a boat
in the sea
in flame!

Stork…Triangle…of legs.

Eye
of a drunkard. Swims
in his glass.

Lying in the boat.
A wave
splashes the star.

Lying
on the grass. An unmown
sky.

The Best of Mijikai Haiku 2013

Traci Siler

Shaking moonbeams
from my hair

The days
when I am not myself
cocoon

Morning moon
clipped fingernail

Warm thunder
sweet
wet rain

Luna Moth
flutter on my lips

Ronit Mitchell

diary
pressed rose
forgotten

his hand
wine on the table
my knee

wild iris
over and over
--our kiss

summer getaway--
feet break free
of socks

Chris Ziesler

flour-fine snow …
diamond dust
air-borne

after snow ...
silence
falls

June rain ..
girl in red wellies
puddlejump!

road-side grave ...
a thrush sings
evensong

Kath Abela Wilson

winter wind
my wish to save each petal

keeping at it
all night
emptying branch

lotus pose
I sit a little taller

green tea and toast
the sound
of wild parrots

heartwood
how I feel his support

Gary Blankenship

dreaming of
an undreamed haiku

never watered
dusty plastic daisies

of an age
my mind believes
it isn't

the comfort
of clover and you

morning moon
doves coo
from every tree

Julian O'Dea

hailstones
melt ...
memories

butterfly
past my face ...
life

becoming
a statue ...
old man

cat
bed
peace

John McDonald

fog -
horn
fugue

snails'
(con)trails

web
fingerprinting
the mist

grinning pumpkins
waiting
for darkness

Steve Wilkinson

December rain
too cold to care

lost cat
paw prints remain

crooked tree
beneath it
a scarecrow's hat

snowy field
two crows become eyes

falling leaf
free at last

Angelo B. Ancheta

moonlight
your bare
essential

night skyline
this madness
in your eyes

biting cold
if I can sing
a ballad

black hole
she blocks me
yet again

Tomislav Maretić (Croatia)

one sound
from a bell-tower...
the silence

spring wind - the whirling elm seeds

elm route –
a bike enters
the seeds' rustle

snow again... different thoughts

backstage – the actor returns to himself

Pat Geyer

mead moon ...
sweet river runs
barefoot

sunset...
sky waits
for moonrise

this moon
with no color
still blue

morning...
night slips off
the dark

Wylanda E. Harris

autumn
one tall tree
ablaze

before dawn
night still wearing
her diamonds

honey moon
crescent almost
touching Earth

windblown
my loose hair
and leaves

Grant Keller

fear flees
love remains
leap - trust in flight

skin
soft and naked
yielding to my touch

our dreams touch
two hearts beat
one-song

no arms
to hold you
words embrace in stead

Ernesto P. Santiago

golden dawn
on the rise-
the black sea

after it rains
the earth smells
of fishes

full moon...
sniffing each other
spawning

bullied;
in His Highness
the frog croaks

N.E. Taylor

random
marigolds
autumn sun

fresh magic
hummingbird
silhouette

noon
two dragonflies
dancing

i am never
who you think
old tree

Davida Luminabes

even with thunderclouds
hummingbirds play

caught by flashlight
thunderstorm frog

through darkness
birds listen
to moon-speak

over our canoe
geese cross full moon

rivers are freezing
little-bear moon

Mark E. Brager

squinting
violets too violet

stillness . . .
dawn's white breath

colder . . .
a distant bell
clearer

snowmelt . . .
a river stone holds
stillness

morning moon . . .
this dew also
fleeting

Freddy Ben-Arroyo

your place
or mine? -
new moon

time stands still empty church

no penguins
in zoo pool-
a snail

birds
in and out -
seasons

her wrinkled blouse blushing smiley face

Ed Bremson is an award winning haiku poet. He earned his BA in Philosophy from North Carolina State University, and his MFA in Creative Writing from National University. He has been writing and publishing poems for fifty years. In 2014 he had a full-length book collection of poetry published, and he also edited a book of Mongolian haiku that was published in Mongolia. Ed lives in Raleigh, North Carolina.

www.ingramcontent.com/pod-product-compliance
Lightning Source LLC
Chambersburg PA
CBHW051045030426
42339CB00006B/207